SOCIAL MEDIA MARKETING

21 POWERFUL MARKETING TIPS TO HELP SKYROCKET TRAFFIC, ESTABLISH AUTHORITY AND BUILD MEDIA PLATFORM FOR YOUR BUSINESS

ENTREPRENEUR PUBLISHING

COPYRIGHT

DISCLAIMER

Your Free Gift

As a special Thank You for downloading this book I have put together an exclusive report on Morning Habits.

Learn how to build your own morning routine to achieve increased productivity and less stress. Includes sample morning routines and exclusive tips towards creating your own.

>> You Can Download This Free Report By Clicking Here <<

FREE GIFT

Kindle 5 Star Books

Free Kindle 5 Star Book Club Membership

Join Other Kindle 5 Star Members Who Are Getting Private Access To Weekly Free Kindle Book Promotions

Get free Kindle books

Stay connected:

Join our Facebook group

Follow Kindle 5 Star on Twitter

Also, if you want to receive updates on Entrepreneur Publishing's new books, free promotions and Kindle countdown deals sign up to their New Release Mailing List.

For entrepreneurs: http://www.entrepreneurfinesse.com

TABLE OF CONTENTS

INTRODUCTION

For any businessman or woman trying to get their products and services out there, advertising and marketing are the two main avenues to go. With the development of social media as a platform for marketing, people now have a multitude of choices when it comes to branding on the Internet. Platforms like Facebook, Twitter, Instagram, Pinterest and Google Plus have millions, even billions of users. Imagine if you could establish authority in a place with an audience all over the world. The best thing about Social Media is that *people are telling you* what they want, like and abhor.

Social Media has taken over computers, cell phones and tablet devices. In many ways it has replaced older forms of communication – phone, email, radio, TV. The best part of all is that using them and building a media platform is free.

In this book you will learn some of the vital and key tips of how to skyrocket your traffic, establish authority online and even how to build a media platform for your online business. You will discover things that help you grow your business when followed appropriately and how to use these tips effectively.

CHAPTER 1
HOW TO SKYROCKET YOUR ONLINE TRAFFIC

If you are starting your business or even if you have been in business for a while and you are now looking to expand your traffic in order to increase your Return on Investment (ROI). With the growth in technology, you can now be able to market you business to millions and all at no cost. All you need is to know how to navigate the vastness of the web, once you are able to do that there is no limit to the number of people you will get into contact with.

In this book you will be able to learn tips on how to increase your traffic using social media for marketing. The lessons will be divided into three chapters each covering a major section of the message behind the idea of the book.

When going into social media marketing, you first have to establish the niche that you are interested in. It is imperative that you have a specific one so that you are able to focus all your energy and time to achieving the best possible results. Here are the seven tips on how to improve and even skyrocket your websites traffic. You should choose a niche that you want to be well identified with.

1. SPYING ON MARKETING COMPETITORS
It would be a wise move to first scrutinize the marketing strategy that is being used by your competitors on the social media community. When you join the social media community so as to find people to convert into your visitors and hopefully your customers, you will find that your competitors are there too. For a beginner, or even businessman who has been in the business for some time, this is a blessing in disguise. First study your enemies and potential customers. Study on how your target audience does things online, how they write their posts, things that they like and even what they share, and then try to mimic that. You should also study how your competitors carry out their jobs online and use that to make yourself even more desirable to consumers.

2. BLOG
When you decide to do your marketing on social media, you should know that the content that you post should be of great quality and is very essential. You should start a blog and ensure that whatever you talk of on the social media networks has a hyperlink leading the reader back to

your blog where you put more information on the topic. For you to attract and maintain visitors on your blog you need to have great and relevant, but also easy to read and understand content. To ensure that your blog is as effective as it could ever be, follow the points given below:

- **Type of Content**
  When it comes to the type of content on your site, make sure that you have the best, informative and easy to understand information. When you go online to look for information, you are not looking to go and start deciphering anything; you just want something that you will easily understand and has informing content.

- **Regularity**
  For any blog to be able to attract visitors and keep them coming back having great content doesn't totally help you, you need to be able to at least blog once or twice a week. If you find that you at times go for weeks without blogging, and then know that you will most definitely lose most of your visitors gained through blogging.

- **Target Audience**
  If you have more than one types of content that you want the online visitors to learn about, you can use different accounts for different content. This way you are able to manage and grow each account with the sole purpose of selling a certain single product.

- **The Content**
  Things you should have covered for the content include such a thing as the person who creates it and the ways in which you plan to promote it. It is okay to hire outside help in coming up with the content in case you are not well versed with the topic at hand.
  You should also find some ways such as attaching their hyper links into comments you make on other blogs or even Facebook and Twitter. This will generate some increased visits to your blog, especially if your comment was well written.

3. BUILD A SOCIAL PRESENCE

When you are looking to create your online social presence, you need to first come up with goals and establish your objectives. When you are building a social media marketing account on Facebook, Twitter, Pinterest or even Instagram, you need to follow the following to ensure that you hit the right target that you are aiming at. These are points that your goals should have in order to simplify the process:

- **Specific**

  You need to have goals that are specific and not all rounded; this will enable you to get more and relevant information instead of having information about everything all at the same time.

- **Measurable**

  Your goals should not be such that you are not able to measure them.   When you are able to measure your goals, it makes it easier for you to plan on how to execute them and even able to break it down into small parts so that you are able to measure the far you have gone and the part you are still to work on. This will motivate you while at work, when you see the much you have covered, you get motivated to complete the remaining parts.

- **Attainable**

  It is okay to be ambitious when setting your goals or even when   working, but you should never make or set goals that you will not be able to achieve. Having big dreams is not a bad thing, it is just more easier to achieve what you are working on if you keep seeing improvements along the way, goals that are not attainable will make you lose hope once you notice that you are not making any development in that front.

- **Relevant**

  As you have already read several times on this book already, finding   the niche that will best express your points and give you the online presence you deserve. Focus on a relevant topic so that you do not end up wasting your time with trying to focus on many ideas at the same time. Relevancy can range from you to the consumer and even the distributor at times. Making the content on your website relevant to all those who visit and your target is a way of getting you repeat visits from the people who visit.

- **Time-bound**

  You should come up with ideas that are time bound in the sense that   you can easily work on tasks based on certain periods of time. This means that you come up with goals that are achievable in given periods of time. This is a very effective way of keeping yourself and anyone else that you might be working with, motivated.

You should also make sure that the story that you tell in your website, is unique and targeted to a given audience. When you visit a website as a potential customer, you will be attracted to visit that site again based on how interesting and informative you found it. A social media page or a website could be very informative but if the visitor is not comfortable while accessing the information, or it is delivered in such a serious tone, there are very many visitors who will not revisit such a site. Online reading is meant to be fun and easy to understand not super complicated, no one is looking to be amazed buy your jargon of the English language.

4. HOST GOOGLE+ HANGOUTS

When looking to skyrocket you online presence, there are very many things that you can do to achieve this goal, it all depends on what works for you. Hosting hangouts on Google+ goes a very long way in creating you an easy platform for you to demonstrate your products. With one on one chats and group chats, you will end up creating a good relationship with your potential customers. If you are really good at conversing and connecting with people, you will not only have one time customers, but will create a good list of repeat customers.

- **Think about your audience first**
  When you plan on hosting a hangout, make sure you understand the needs and wants of your audience. Make the topics appealing and ensure that your audience has the right to dictate what they want to read and what they don't.

- **End Goals**
  With end goals being specific you will be able to find out the return on investment of each hangout. Having specific goals is a good thing since it motivates you to keep going when you see what you have achieved and what is left to be done.

- **Conversation Angle**
  When you are addressing your readers on your blog, you should make sure to approach topics in a way that stands out from the rest. Make sure that you find a great topic and deliver it accordingly. Focus on the keywords in your conversation and your hangout will be at the top on Google.

- **Practice**
  The only sure way of being good at hosting a Google+ hangout is by practicing. When you are looking to master something, you need to keep doing it repeatedly in order to understand it and be able to do it without any difficulties in the future. You will be able to learn even where you can have your videos found. This will also help you in continuously improving your show with time.

- **Scheduling Your Hangout**
  Now that you have done all the preparations, it is time for you to come up with a date and time for broadcasting your hangout. You can schedule you hangout for a certain

future date and have the permanent URLs sent to the people who are to be involved in the hangout.

5. CREATING A BUZZ

With the rate at which technology has developed, we have come from an error where you needed tons of money to be recognized as a brand, to one which you can easily market yourself with no resources at all. Things such as releasing a press release have become very easy to handle and you do not even spend a cent, there are sites that releasing them for you free of charge. If you are looking to create some major buzz online, you can follow these easy steps and you will be well on your way:

- **Creating a Story**
  When you are preparing to make a sale, it is wise that you start with a story that you know the client will relate to. When they hear like the story is about them, you will easily have   a connection and they can buy from you. When you use a true story and make the connection with the client, there are high chances that you will retain him or her for long, just make sure not to make up stories –people tend to tell between true and exaggerated stories.

- **Ask Your Clients for Input**
  When you want to come up with the best selling strategy or you want to make the most buzz, ask the consumers what they like the most and create you product surrounding those answers. Once you understand what your customers want, it will be easy to satisfy their needs, unlike if you had no idea what they needs were. Even when you want to introduce a new product in your line, talk to them and ask them what they think about it.

- **Blogging**
  Every company that is serious on increasing its online buzz and traffic should definitely have a blog. It does not take a lot of time to come up with a post about what your day was like and what you have been up to regarding the production and services offered by your business.

- **Posting Videos on YouTube**
  It is evident that most people prefer watching something more than reading about it, even if it takes a shorter period to read about it than to watch the clip. Most people nowadays use YouTube as a source of information and they go there to search for solutions for their problems. It is imperative that you think of creating testimonial videos –especially ones with some of your clients, this will give you immediate credibility.

- **Article Writing**

  Articles should be written to showcase your expertise in your area of practice. Make sure that you are able to get out as many stories in form of articles as you simply can. Use a tone that will be communicating directly to your consumer and make sure that you touch on the benefits that they will gain by working with you. Constant writing of articles will also make sure that your website always has content, and it also makes it easier for someone to find you.

- **Social Media Networking**

  No matter which one you feel comfortable with, or one that is more relevant to your target audience, just make sure that you are active on social media. Facebook has over 200 million subscribers across the globe, that means if you are advertising on it, you are doing so on a market of over two hundred million people. That is quite a huge audience given that you are not being charged to connect with them.

6. GET ON THE MAP

You should now take advantage of some of the business directories that are for free, it is wise that you first try with the free accounts before making any serious move. If you have been in the business for a while and you are looking to step things up a bit, you need to rebrand yourself and advertise yourself more. Here are a few steps that you should follow:

- **Improving Your Brand's Visibility**

  The use of links or having referrals from previous customers is your best asset. Use SEO techniques to ensure that you come across as a trustworthy person; this will help your visitors like and even trust you. Once you are trusted by your visitors you will be on a stage where you will start to get many referrals. You should also use links within your great content to ensure that when people such for you in Google they get results with a story about you and your business. The link can be of either an article or even a video you have on YouTube talking about your products and services.

- **Web Design**

  The appearance of your website could tell more about yourself, if you have an old site or if you are just starting out, you need a great site. The website you use should reflect the clientele that you are catering for. If you have a website that looks like a high school project or one that lacks in class and allure, you need to change and come up with an awesome design that reflects your target audience.

- **Social Media**

  You should be able to amplify and manage your social media accounts. You should be able to set up your own profiles and also train your team so that they can work for you as you check on them to ensure that they do the jobs okay. The social media platform can enable you to access tens of thousands of people that you couldn't have otherwise reached. You can easily amplify the number of people you want to see your products, events and even services that you offer.

- **Search Engine Optimization**
  This can be defined as the process of one getting their website to the of search engines -a natural, un-paid and organic section. You can easily buy your way to the top with buying of the ads, but most people do not read the ads but look on the natural section. A person, who is on top of the unpaid section, is one who deserves it and not because of how much money he might have.

You can also give some offers to your existing customers for products with others that complement them. If you only have one product, you can get in contact with a business that offers products that complement yours. You are to make a deal with such a company and boost up your sales and in the process creating some buzz all around.

Including testimonials in your site will give you a lot of credibility. You need all the credibility you can get and hopefully it is transformed into a referral. You should link to sites such as Google and Yelp in order to prove your credibility on your site.

7. CREATE VALUABLE PRODUCT

This should not need any reminding but since it's a vital part of the process, I thought it wise to share it with you. A business could have all the attention in the whole business world, but if the products that it produces are below the normal measure of quality, you can rest assured that it will not be making any positive buzz. There are some ways that you can use to make your products value grows and they include:

- **Skipping the Long Features**
  Listen to your clients and figure out what is important to each and design your product in such a way that they satisfy the needs of your customers. Avoiding using long features could save you buyers because most people are not looking for products that are presented in a complex way.

- **Get the People Talking**
  The more that your product is talked about, the more valuable it seems and thus will bring in a high profit. When you ensure that you customers are happy with your services you can then ask them to tell some of their friends. You can even have some of your customer's testimonials on your social media page and have the potential customers see how you conduct your business.

- **Test Drive**

  People like to test products before they buy to ensure that they are buying the genuine product. When you have people trying your products risk free, you create confidence in your customers and that will make them very loyal. When integrates with your product through testing, he or she is much more obliged to buy the product.

- **Ease of Use**

  Online consumers are mainly there to look for easy and quick solutions to their problems, the easier you make your product, the more value it will have in your customer's eyes. Also offering some training on the product is a much better way of selling it for it simplifies the understanding of the customer. The offering of training in person will get you more sales than just packaging a product with a user manual in it. The uneducated people would opt for the option that includes a tutor and not just a paper they can't even read.

If you are new to the online selling of products and services, it is advisable that you start out small and grow your way up. Taking a minimalistic approach is a very good way of starting out your business to first assess the market and gauge the response. You should also write some eBooks on topics related to your blog, you will find that most people like detailed and easy to understand information.

CHAPTER 2
ESTABLISHING AUTHORITY ONLINE

When you establish yourself as an authority to reckon with online, there are some benefits that will come with that. Establishing yourself as credible, resourceful and legitimate source of information is very important for an online trader. Some of the benefits that you will get from gaining online authority include:

- You will be able to generate more sales as a result of quickly gained trust from your customers and the prospects.

- Partnerships and opportunities are very important to the growth of a business; all you have to do is establish some respect among your peers.

- This way you will be able to attract many offline and even online referrals.

- You can easily reduce the startup costs of marketing by getting tractions on ventures on projects in a more efficient manner.

- Authority can turn you into a big source for a certain industry thus causing your website or blog receive lots of traffic.

The creation of authority online is helpful in more than just creating strong ties with the readers, but also pushes the writer to come up with high quality content for it will be associated with his or her name.

Building Authority Online

Authority in whatever field or situation that it is applied can lead to production of some the best desired products that the consumers could ever want. Authority will help you attract traffic, establish ranking and even generate some meaningful conversations. If you are not that much of a leader you can easily change that by reading and mastering the following characteristics:

- **Content**
  You can never compromise on quality when it comes to content, you should have a specific way of formatting your content. Also have a specific number of words that will be in each blog. Ensure that the content is aimed at a target audience of a certain age group and from a certain location.

- **Social**

  Look at your previous posts on the social media networks that you are apart of, how well are they doing. What number and type of shares do you get, is your post actively used in conversations and how good is your follower base, is it a number of enough people to sustain your business or do you need to increase it.

- **Links**

  When you are writing online and you have your own blog/website, you want to make sure that anyone that you attract is able to access you. This is where URLs and hyperlinks come in, use a number of links that is enough to attract attention but not too much to outdo the content written.

- **Offline**

  You should also cover bases such as the internal network; engage in speaking with consumers and future prospects. You should also consider sponsorships from big companies or other forms of investors.

- **Recognition**

  To appear more credible can get you the authority that you are looking for online. Use of citations and mentions as well as previous consumer's testimonials can lead to good generation of recognition among consumers and peers in the same industry.

Here are the next six steps in the 21 tips of getting your business to skyrocket and also building authority online. The following are seven tips of showing you how you can easily generate authority online:

8. CONTENT

To establish yourself as an online authority you need to be producing content on a regular basis and make sure that you use it properly. To ensure that your content is helpful and can give you the authority that you are looking for, you need to follow the following tips:

Start a niche focused blog: When you start this form of blog, you will be able to focus on one niche and understand it thoroughly, this will give you all the knowledge you would require being an online authority in that particular niche. Since you will be well versed with the niche you will be able to answer any questions directed your way by any consumer and this could increase your credibility as opposed to someone who is trying to work on four or five niches at the same time.

- **Optimizing and Updating**

  For you to be able to become an online authority figure, you need to first put your business in order. Updating your old content and other website information, as well as optimizing your website will give credibility. A business that does not update their website and blogs are rarely used for they are taken to be dormant and the business closed.

- **Evergreen Content**
  This is content that is intended to remain relevant for long periods of time, therefore, when writing them quality should be highly considered. For you to come up with the best evergreen articles you need to abide to the following five tips:

- **Know the Audience**
  When writing this kind of content it is wise to assume that the reader searching for the article is a beginner in that particular field. With that in mind, you will be able to write the article without lots of complicated jargon and make it very easy to understand, yet informative.

- **Research on Your Keyword**
  When you focus on a broad approach of content you risk having lengthy articles that may be too general for them to get any online exposure. Make sure that you research well your keywords to be able to come up with good and relevant content. Look for a keyword phrase for your article and stick to that, give precise information and not general stuff.

- **Linking Everything**
  The evergreen content that you come up with will best suit novices, this means that there is room for more improvement and more research to get the article more detailed and advanced. Link them back to your more high level work to ensure that all your work is available no matter where the consumer looks for it from.

- **Establishing Your Headline**
  It is wise that you avoid titles that may not generate traffic, making sure that your article is keyword centric and narrowly focused will lead to more traffic and ease of creating your page and URLs.

- **Lifespan of Your Content**
  When it comes to evergreen content, some can have a limited lifespan. Knowing which contents have limited lifespan ahead of time will help you come up with the most efficient URL structure that will easily allow opportunities for additional content.

- **Regular Blogging**
  To ensure that your content is selling, you need to be in a point where you are always producing and pushing content. Ensure that the quality of the articles that you produce is

high and then come up with a calendar that will have you publishing content on a regular basis.

- **Curate Content**
  To curate content is to simply come up with information based on content that is already online. Anyone can come up with content but not everyone can come up with effective content. Effective content is one that is made up of opinions, information, humor, news and controversy to produce results and help in the growth of a business both offline and online.

How to Find Content to Curate
For you to start curating you need to first find discover the best content to use. You do not want to spend most of your time online away from your business, you are looking for some good content to work with and be able to blend both your job and your life. Given below are some ways of finding the right content to curate:

- **Google+ Communities**
  Finding communities that are broadcasting content in your field of interest will at times help you find some information that you might want to use. Although you can get information and use it right on Google+ feed, make sure that you do not let your profile become too noisy. Too much noise on your profile will contribute in the reduction of your visitors. The Google+ communities maybe new and young in the market but they are becoming important sources of useful information.

- **LinkedIn News**
  Through the use of sharing information through the LinkedIn news section, they have been able to provide a platform on which you can easily get great information.

- **Google**
  Doing a Google blog search with the industry you are looking for as the topic, you will be able to see the blogs that are consistent on the first Google page. You can use the information from the articles appearing consistently on your Google first page. If you are focusing on a narrow niche, use the title and the name blog at the end.

- **Twitter**
  This is one of the underestimated but yet very useful tool for finding content to curate. You can simply use all the tools offered on this social network, to find content that is great. You can use hash tags, discover users and even trends to find some of the great content of your specific industry.

- **Alltop**

  You can also search for your relevant industry and categories of the content that you are looking for. Alltop allows submissions and yet still, their directories are very well on point and they offer you the best sites and blogs with the highest quality.

- **Online Publications**

  When you are able to find new and relevant content in popular websites and blogs, you stand a better chance of coming across the source of content relevant to you.

- **Other Curators**

  If you are new to the field of content curating and you are looking to discover some new content, then you can study the other curators. This is the best form of education in which you observe and imitate. Look for sites that are specifically created for the sole purpose of curating content. Buzzfeed is a good example of such sites in which your can easily find the services of a curator.

How to Curate Content

Content curating is a process in which new content is derived from already used content. There are several ways of learning how to curate content.

- **Social Bookmarking App**

  Social bookmarking app such as Reddit, StumbleUpon, Instapaper, Delicious and Pocket among others is highly recommended when you are reading online. They are simple, able to tag, sharing features and multi-device support app is very useful especially when you do not have time to catch up on whatever is going on at the moment. It helps you save the page and you can easily access it when you are not busy.

- **IFTTT**

  Using IFTTT you can easily automate the curation process as much as you possibly can. This is an automatic tool that allows you to use custom recipes to perform some tasks automatically. If you are one of those people who favorite post on twitter to read it later, but always tend to forget, using an IFTTT can help you receive reminders on your Evernote or Google reader.

- **ShowYou**

  If you are more into finding information to curate through videos, and then the use of ShowYou has proved to be very informative and entertaining. Other than pulling videos from all your favorite sites, it can also help save videos that have content that you want to curate later.

- **Google Drive**
  If you are one of the many people who love having their information arranged in spreadsheets, Google Drive is the best move for your. You can simply input the links and articles manually or just employ the services of the IFTTT explained above.

- **RSS Reader**
  Although it is viewed as a dying technology, RSS is still a very good source of great content for curating. Subscribing to RSS feeds that are of your interest industry, will see you receive some informative and great content to work with.

9. SOCIAL

When you are trying to gain some authority, no matter the capacity, you need to be able to connect with people. It would be hard for you to communicate your plans of running for office if you are not comfortable talking to people. You can leverage social media to your own advantage and in gaining authority by doing the following:

- **Establishing a Social Following**
  If you are looking to have some major authority online you need to establish some serious social following of follower s who are receptive and an engaged audience. There are several ways of enabling you to establish some meaningful social following, they include:

- **Understanding Why and What you're Building**
  Understanding what you are trying to build and why it is necessary to your business is one sure way of coming up with a strong social following. Ensure that your social community is one that is fond of communicating; communication brings about the quick and organic growth of a community.

- **A Plan**
  Trying to attack the problem of social media without any sound plan is like going on a suicide mission. It is a very regular occurrence in which we see a businessman start engaging himself with online marketing and then a few months down the line, they just quit with no warning.

- **Following Etiquette**
  You should first and foremost know that not all trends are favorable, also learn on when to properly leverage anything that you get. Bad etiquette or manners can see you lose large numbers of visitors in very short spans of time. Find out about a trend

before you try and use it to try and gain more visitors, especially from an audience that you know nothing about.

- **Being Receptive, Caring and Real**
  If you are looking to expand your number of visitors, you will need to find out how to join their channels. Make it possible for you and your customers to communicate online –answer to their comments, ensure that your answers are pretty helpful and that your comments are genuine.

- **Sticking to a Schedule**
  If you want to have a successful social media, you need to plan your schedule such that it is easy to follow. It is common to here of a great idea that cannot be reached due to the fact that the schedule was not followed. The advantage of schedules is that they help plan ahead and this goes a long way in preventing the occurrence of unexpected things.

- **Customize Your Social Media Pages**
  Attracting visitors to your website simply by how you have designed it, the content you post and how you handle it in general can be an added advantage towards getting authority. If you decide to use social media marketing, be ready to spend some money on the appearance of your website and blog.

- **Paid Advertising**
  You can also take advantage of the paid advertisements. These will gain you some quick recognition in no time. Since all you need for this is money, you can easily move your position further up.

- **Networking**
  When you are on social media and you are looking for some credibility in order to come up with some authority, you need to get in touch and connect with some of the big names in the field of your interest. Building of good relationships with such people will see you get exposure to more and more people especially those who follow the ones you have befriended.

- **Consistent Schedule**
  When it comes to the acquiring of authority online, you cannot simply do it by just coming and posting one great article or even a video and then disappearing and still hope to gain authority, You will need to be consistent in your endeavor and ensure

that you keep your name and products in the mind of the consumer by ensuring you repeatedly post relevant and informative content.

10. LINKS

Google has no plans of removing the use of links, not even after they introduce the Author Rank –this is an app made by Google to ensure that an author is credited for the job they do online, so it is imperative that you keep working on your links so as to reap as many benefits as you possibly can, here are some of the ways that links can bring your authority:

- When you are providing guest post on sites that are into the same niche are you are. You just drop in a link in a strategic point to ensure you that the people who come by and agree with your points of the discussion, can find more on your site by following the link.

- You should also be friendly to the editors and journalists in your niche of interest so that you at times get editorial links. Editorial links are very important for they will get you more coverage than you can come up with in your early ages of building authority.

- You can also attract links from other sites and blogs by simply using content marketing –use of content in a creative and consistent manner in the aim of integrating companies with their online strategies.

- You can also add value to blogs by just making some helpful and meaningful comments from time to time. Having people recognize you for the quality and consistent contribution to such conversations creates curiosity which ends up with the readers looking for the source.

- Engage your followers in small games where they can win an embeddable badge when they achieve a certain score. This keeps your visitors motivated and always eager to participate.

11. OFFLINE

Online strategies are not the only ways that you can use to build authority, there is quite a number of things that you can do offline that can result in the growth of your online authority. Things such as building relationships and even social sharing that happen among such relationships can assist in authority building. Some of the offline strategies include:

- When you find a group of people discussing topics that are in line with your niche of interest, you can join them and contribute towards the conversation. This way you will be able to get hold of both online and offline followers who will then be a part of the growing authority you are trying to build online.

- Throwing small parties or cocktail hours right before a meeting are other effective ways of gaining authority. When people are relaxed and feeling free, it is easier to get to them and make them see some points in your line of view, you will easily connect to people when they are having cocktails or in a party unlike if you were in an office.

- You can also sponsor someone else's conference, this way you will be able to meet with all the vital and important people who show up. You will be in a good position to converse with them and even get them to follow you on social media if they are interested in the niche industry that you work on.

- You can also gain some recognition by running a charity event, this way you get to connect with a large group of professionals from the niche you are fascinated by and you also help the less fortunate.

- You can also engage in hosting meet ups where you invite speakers who specialize in the same field as the one that you work in. This is bound to create some buzz in the industry and you will be the center of attention for sometime –this is very imperative for it will bring you more traffic in a very short duration of time.

12. RECOGNITION

One of the most efficient and easiest way of gaining authority online is by having lots of recognition from sources that matter. If you are then able to ensure that the recognition holds, you will be in a great position to garner all the authority you want online. Here are some of the simple and yet effective ways to achieve this:

- You can do this by first visiting sites such as LinkedIn and Angie's List and collecting all the endorsements you can simply get. The better your followers know you, the more they are going to endorse you on the LinkedIn and the more recognition you will rake up. This feature has not been on LinkedIn for a long time but for the short time that it has been around, it has raised the standards of people on the site.

- If you are on sites such as Yelp, Google+ Places or any other of the like, you can gain some recognition by earning positive testimonials and reviews from some of your past and present consumers. These reviews and testimonials are what give you some credibility and this leads to you gaining some recognition online.

- When you find some online competitions on the niche of your interest, make sure that you submit some content in order to win the prizes. Even when you do not win anything you still get your name out there and a chance for people to recognize you. It is even better when you win the competition.

- The best way of all is to become an industry source providing editors with soundbites and quotes to use for their articles. This is a sure way to gain some recognition and provided you keep your end of the deal, the editors will get your recognized in many places than you had estimated.

- Ensuring that everyone who visits your page or profile knows exactly who you are, make sure that you post all your certifications and degrees in your bio. The better people think they know you, the more they will be willing to support and even believe things you say online.

13. MOBILE PHONES

The thing about mobile phones is that they are now being used by almost everyone in the world. If as a blogger ore a social media marketer, have a website or blog that is on a platform that is not accessible by the phone you need to think again.

There are whispers about Google locking out and penalizing all those with websites that cannot be accessed via the smart phones. A very large percentage of people access online information through their phones and as an online marketer you should capitalize on that. If you are looking to create some serious authority online, you need to be accessible on all platforms with ease.

This form of marketing is one in which ads appear on Smartphones, tablets and other mobile devices. Since all mobile devices offer different and function on different media platforms, you should find a way to customize and format your ads that they are compatible with all the platforms available.

The mobile devices are taking the place of computers at a very fast speed, the following are some statistics that were carried out in respect to finding out how the mobile Smartphones are performing.

- More than 40% of the time spent on the internet is done through mobile devices.
- Around seventy percent of more web pages are viewed on tablets as opposed to those on the Smartphone.
- Eighty percent of the time spent on apps is majorly spent on game apps, and thus it is wise to include ads on the game apps.
- In the year 2012 the searches in mobile devices had increased by a two hundred percent margin.

The use of mobile devices is here to stay and for a person looking to get some authority online, you should always know where the tide is going.

Some of the ways that you can use the mobile marketing strategy to get authority online include:

a. **In-game Mobile Marketing**
this involves the popping up of ads or even banners in the games advertising for a certain company. They can also appear in between loading pages, they are effective since the user cannot avoid viewing them.

b. **Location-based Marketing**
These are very effective ways of advertising in which the mobile ads are designed and set to appear only when the mobile user is in a certain geographical region. Some businesses like the idea of the consumer getting an alert of their ads only when they are close to their business' operations area.

c. **Mobile Image Ads**
These are image ads specifically designed to appear on mobile devices in order to create awareness about something, Using images ads on mobile devices is quite a clever way since most people use their mobile devices to log on into the internet.

d. **QR Codes**
These are codes that you scan with your mobile device and it takes you to a location that is attached to the codes. This takes you to places that you have no idea of and in a way expands your knowledge and recognition online.

e. **App-based Marketing**
You have read that 80% of the time spent on mobile devices goes on game app, you do not have to create your own game to get the recognition you need. There are apps that are free online and are designed to put your add in a third party's game. Apps such as Facebook has very many ads integrated in its feeds that most of the time the user does not realize when they are viewing an advert.

f. **Mobile Search Ads**
These are similar to the ones that you will find online of Google, only that these are designed to be compatible with a phone to the extent that you can just press and option on the screen and directly contact the business.

g. **SMS**

When you are using the mobile platform to reach your customers, you will also get their phone numbers in the process and you can send them messages about products that you think they might be interested in.

That is the last point in the process of creating some authority online; the next thing that we are going to be discussing is the tips of how you will be able to come up with your own media platform for your business.

CHAPTER 3
BUILDING A MEDIA PLATFORM FOR YOUR ONLINE BUSINESS

Once you have achieved the first two endeavors, the completion of this third one will not be that much of a problem. Building a platform that will enable the system of your business to function even when you are not around, can be termed as success. The process in which one used to work for a whole day and get minimal returns on what they invest, are well past, with the availability of systems that can assist in helping you build a platform that can operate your business on your behalf you will be able to sleep knowing that your business is still being taken care of. We all get twenty four hours in a day and how we decide to leverage and spend that time is up to us. It would be wise to work smart for some hours than work hard all day long and with minimal returns.

The following are the remaining tips in the 21 that you were promised at the beginning of this book. Make sure that you follow them all to the letter if you are looking for them to help you out in any way.

As a new business in the industry, if you are looking to make an online media platform you will need to approach the subject in a more informed and lightly way. There are steps that you can take to ensure that you gain the platform that you are looking for, they include the following:

14. BEING OF SERVICE
When you are starting out online it is wise that you be of use and help to others online. It might be consuming your time but as long as you are interacting with other people and getting your name out there, you are okay. Reaching out to help others is a very sure way of ensuring that others reach out to help you when in need.

Being of free services, makes you come into contact with some of your future clients and even helps you get the know, like and trust that you need from your visitors online. You can engage with them too by sharing bits of tips and opinions that you know are useful to them, this will attract them to you as a business.

There are two groups of people that you will be looking to connect that will need your help, this includes the potential clients and the other business owners. Write blogs, ask the customers what they want, share their stuff online and even reach out your followers, in this way you are able to help the potential and other business owners and make yourself known to them.

15. CULTIVATE A COMMUNITY
The use of social media has made it possible that you can easily create a community around your

business. This is one way of nurturing a consumer tribe which is a group of consumers who are loyal to a certain brand, business or product.

When you are rewarding the community members for their loyalty and even engage with them, you can also encourage them to share their experiences. This will lead to some improvement in your business; it will also play a role in giving your customers and followers some sense of identity, which makes them feel invested in the business.

16. MAINTAINING CONSISTENCY
When you are new to the online business and you are looking to build your own platform. It is smart that once you start your own site, you do not do things halfheartedly. When it comes to posting of blogs, make sure that they are consistent and that they make some sense in the way they follow one another. Also you should keep the consistency of the voice of your brand and the message consistency.

This is a factor that you should be very keen on if you have more than one source posting on behalf of your business. If you can only operate with several outlet sources, make sure that you bring them together and agree on the voice that the brand should carry.

Ensure that you at least post once a week, but daily engagement on the social networks media will make it easier for you to come up with a media platform on which you can conduct your online business.

17. PUBLISHING OF TIMELY AND RELEVANT CONTENT
There are two groups of content that you can post on social media, they include blog posts, testimonials and videos created by your business or you can use content that was created by some other business. Using both of the sources is advisable as it will create relevance to your fanbase.

You can be sharing news stories that are relevant to the state of the consumers at the time that you are writing your blog. You can write an article about plumbing and drainage fixing, right after a storm that left some drains blocked and homes flooded.

The ability to share stories that are relevant to the consumer's right at the time that they are reading the content is a smart move. If you offer the solution for the problem that might be happening, advertise as you are ready to go to work, make sure that you offer great services such that the customer will want to have you serve them again.

18. MAKE A PLAN FOR YOUR SOCIAL MEDIA
Before you start on anything, it is always important that you ask yourself what you are about to do and whether it is beneficial to you in any way or not. Planning will help you eliminate activities that are not beneficial to you and your business. Having a well defined plan on what you plan on achieving by using the social media for marketing. Good ideas of what you are

looking to accomplish will guide you into building your own social media platform on which you will be able to conduct your business.

The first thing that you should do when planning about your first media platform is define your goals, both short and long term. Decide whether you want to be alerting consumers of upcoming deals, building an engaged community online or generating leads by driving social traffic to your site, and when you decide on which one, stick to that one throughout.

Being able to keep the guidelines will help you manage maneuvering in the social media and keep you a float for longer. The better you study and understand and the guidelines, the easier it will be for you to come up with a great social media platform.

19. ESTABLISHING YOURSELF ON A SOCIAL PLATFORM

If you are looking for a great media platform for your business you can start by being able to define your brands identity. Once you are able to tie together your marketing and brand strategy with your social media, you will have made a very bold move towards identifying yourself on the social media.

When you are using photos, descriptions, logos and business information, make sure that these are always consistent across all the social platforms that you can be found on. It is not wise to use images and logos that are different across several social media accounts that belong to the same business. You would be better of coming up with an image and logo that you will always be using rather than having to use different photos that have nothing in common.

Also, have content that is always consistent will play a role in giving your customers a stronger sense of the message you are sending out there. It makes it much easier for you consumers to see how your business is going to help them fulfill a certain need that they happen to have.

20. BRAND MAPPING

When it comes to creating your own online media platform, it is essential that you do some brand mapping, this helps you plan on what tools that you will use and how you will use them. The basic brand mapping includes two products from different brands but offering the same services placed against their prices, this is use to determine which product is more efficient and is fair on the price.

You can easily use brand mapping to set yourself aside from the competition by learning their strengths and weaknesses and then using that against him or her. To improve more you should take the attributes of your business, areas of weakness and attributes that you can work on to become stronger. These attributes include things such as price of goods and even the performance of employees.

Then make sure that when you come to producing products, ensure that you follow your branding map and that way you will be able to reach out to consumers that might have liked your brand mapping.

21. COME UP WITH A CHECKLIST

Once you have decided that you are going to be focusing on using your social media to make some income, thing of the tools and sites that you can use to achieve you goals. You can deliver your content through all the channels that you may know you can even find someone good with video and have them make you a nice video to share on YouTube.

Make a list of tools and types of content to use and then narrow it down to what you will need and use only. Make sure that you cover all the bases from people who like watching, reading to those who love to listen.

Also get some sort of a social media management tool this will help you be able to manage all your social media accounts. This is one important tool that you must have especially if you are dealing with several accounts.

The tips that you have been reading have been complied together so that they may be used in assisting people to improve their online experience and gain some authority and even build some platforms for their businesses in the process. They might have been few in numbers but the knowledge that they carry with them is enough to help you achieve and answer all the questions that led you to this book.

Conclusion

I hope this book was able to help you to realize all the information that you must have been looking for in order to improve your online marketing. All the work that you will have accomplished by the end of this book is not really worth it if you are not able to tell just how much you have accomplished. You have covered all the angles in which a person can possibly learn about growing authority online and even building their own business platform.

Make sure that you remember to enable all your websites such that they can be accessed through the phones, as I earlier told you, Google is planning on shutting out the sites that are not compatible with the mobile devices.

Also as you work on your marketing do not be scared of by the fact that it looks complicated, it is actually a very easy thing to learn. It is the part in which you get to announce to many people – both strangers and friends, and let them know that you have started a business.

To hear about Entrepreneur Publishing's new books first (and to be notified when there are free promotions), sign up to their New Release Mailing List.

Finally, if you enjoyed this book, please take the time to share your thoughts and post a review on Amazon. It'd be greatly appreciated!

Thank you and good luck!

Preview Of 'Video Marketing: How To Produce Viral Films And Leverage Facebook, YouTube, Instagram And Twitter To Build A Massive Audience' from Entrepreneur Publishing

STEP NUMBER ONE: RELEASE YOUR FOCUS ON QUALITY.

In this chapter, you will learn:

- Getting the best result doesn't need costly investment.
- For videos, the type and purpose define the quality of performance.

QUALITY VIDEO DOESN'T MEAN COSTLY EQUIPMENT.
If you have spent any time at all watching those catchy, interesting, clever 'viral videos', you have seen a wide spectrum of quality, lighting, performance, audio clarity, and other qualifying criteria. Some of the videos are grainy and confusing, others are studio-quality masterworks.

In all frankness, there is no particular level of appropriate quality that ends up as a minimum for the development of a positively catchy and appealing video clip.

CLEAR IMAGES DON'T REQUIRE EXPENSIVE CAMERAS OR LIGHTING.
For this reason, if you have a fairly modern cell phone with a camera, you are probably already set to shoot video. The appeal of both snapshots and short video, for personal, family, and community purposes have led the various producers into a product war of sorts, ensuring just about any camera out there would be sufficient for most tasks. As we proceed, certain situations will present themselves where this may not be the case, but we will deal with those as we find them in the coming chapters.

SOUND, TOO, IS USUALLY MORE THAN ADEQUATE.

Many of the kinds of videos that 'go viral' either have little or no audio characteristics, but even those that do, because again the primary photo and audio device is a phone, the particular sound capture requirements are already adequate for general use. We will cover other particulars in later chapters on this account as well.

KEEP IT CONCISE

"Brevity is the soul of wit." Most of us know almost instinctively that the best of the 'viral videos' out there are short and sweet. Some basic ideas about the very length of the video you might want to create do entail keeping it short. Here are some tips about how to do just that.

CUT TO THE CHASE

When scripting the video, if it is operating as a script, cut out all the lead-in and trailing video, but the scenes you want to remain. Replace long explanatory video with a scrolling text explanation, and run that just before the particular scene. When the video is complete, cut in a scrolling text with your call to action and any explanation you think it needs, as well as concluding with a "Thanks for watching" message.

SUBTITLES GO A LONG WAY.

Often, it is easier to just run a small scrolling text along the top or the bottom of the image, as a means of explaining things to the viewer as that seems to help the continuity flow. If necessary, include some humor or irony in the subtext, to cause them to watch the video more than once.

REALIZE THE BREADTH OF YOUR OPTIONS

At this point, be excited about the potential, and as you read the following sections, your alternatives and options will only improve even more than you may have considered. Remember, the field is really relatively new, and there are a lot of different choices about not only your video subject, but also your video theme, method, angle, etc. Get ready to have a lot of fun!

Keep a Positive, Uplifting, Inspiring theme

Fundamentally, the aspect of videos that drives the almost manic viewing is the ways in which the images and the stories behind them are matters of positive attitude, good stories, and happy endings. Even the stories or images that have a dark or challenging theme tend to be bright, happy imagery.

We all want to win.

By keeping the focus on the positive, you continue the very flow of positivity that brought the viewers to your video. Play that optimism and enthusiasm to its core, and keep the viewer engaged.

One good video leads to another.

When the viewer enjoys one of your videos, it incites them to try another. And another. Keeping that momentum going leads to multiple views, increase engagement, and returning viewers. All lead to more page views, and that can, over time, lead to payoff through the variety of monetizing methods, which we will discuss later.

LIGHT-HEARTED AND EASY TO IDENTIFY WITH EXPERIENCE

Think of your own video-watching. Are you more likely to watch one about a cute animal, or a how-to on flossing your teeth? Sure, we might try to suggest that we think about our dental condition more, but when push comes to shove, the cute sneezing panda or caterwauling panther cub is going to eat up that spare minute. So create your video with an eye to what the viewer desires, and you will be ahead of the game.

EYEBALLS EQUAL SALES

There are two things to remember when creating your video content. The eyes of your target customer. Though we haven't touched on it yet, it is imperative that the attention you draw is turned into a financial benefit. You don't make a video for the sake of having video. You do so to drive the consumer to act, if it is nothing more than watching another video. Because attention is so precious, you never want to give it away without some action you want to be completed.

THE VIEWER IS A BUYER

It may not feel like it, particularly if your message is a 'soft target' – getting the consumer, the viewer to press the 'like' button, or to 'share' the video through social media. Still, whether they are writing the check for the end product, or opening their intellectual wallets by conveying your message on into their networks, the viewer is a customer, and we do well when we remember that.

Click here to check out the rest of Video Marketing: How To Produce Viral Films And Leverage Facebook, YouTube, Instagram And Twitter To Build A Massive Audience on Amazon.

Or go to: http://amzn.to/1y7bm9y

MORE BOOKS FOR ENTREPRENEURS

Click here to check out the rest of Entrepreneur Publishing's books on Amazon.

Below you'll find some of my other popular books that are popular on Amazon and Kindle as well. Simply click on the links below to check them out. Alternatively, you can visit my author page on Amazon to see other work done by me.

How Audiobooks Make You Smarter: 7 Little Known Ways Audio Books Can Boost Memory Capacity And Increase Intelligence

How To Write A Book And Publish On Amazon: Make Money With Amazon Kindle, CreateSpace And Audiobooks

Gardening For Entrepreneurs: Gardening Techniques For High Yield, High Profit Crops

Speed Reading For Entrepreneurs: Seven Speed Reading Tactics To Read Faster, Improve Memory And Increase Profits

Content Marketing Strategies: How Delivering Sensational Value Can Help You Build A Digital Media Empire

Kindle Publishing For Entrepreneurs: 9 Steps To Producing Best Selling Amazon Kindle Books And Building Incredible Passive Income

Video Marketing: How To Produce Viral Films And Leverage Facebook, YouTube, Instagram And Twitter To Build A Massive Audience

If the links do not work, for whatever reason, you can simply search for these titles on the Amazon website to find them.

Preview Of 'Insert Book Title Here'

This section is designed to provide the reader a preview of one of your other books for the assigned pen name. Simply copy and paste a chapter of another book that you have available on Kindle and link to it below.

Click here to check out the rest of (insert book name here) on Amazon.

   If the links do not work, for whatever reason, you can simply search for the pen name of the author or the name of the titles on the Amazon website to find them.

Check Out My Other Books

Below you'll find some of my other popular books that are popular on Amazon and Kindle as well. Simply click on the links below to check them out. Alternatively, you can visit my author page on Amazon to see other work done by me.

-- (Link to your other books here. You can use bit.ly links as well to track the clicks). --

My Other Book - This Is My Other Book On Amazon

My Other Book - This Is My Other Book On Amazon

My Other Book - This Is My Other Book On Amazon

My Other Book - This Is My Other Book On Amazon

My Other Book - This Is My Other Book On Amazon

My Other Book - This Is My Other Book On Amazon

If the links do not work, for whatever reason, you can simply search for these titles on the Amazon website to find them.

www.ingramcontent.com/pod-product-compliance
Lightning Source LLC
Chambersburg PA
CBHW070743180526
45168CB00004B/1518